THE GIFT OF TIME

A SHORT STORY

INCLUDED IN 'YOUR MOTHER'S NIGHTMARES', A COLLECTION OF SIX TROUBLING TALES

ANITHA KRISHNAN

DREAM PEDLAR BOOKS

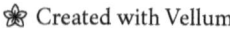

For Dhruv,
the greatest miracle in my life.
How lucky am I to have realized what makes my time on earth so
valuable! It's your presence in my life, above all. Thank you for
giving me the privilege of being your mother in this lifetime.

∾

ABOUT THIS BOOK

The Gift Of Time

Time! Ah, that slippery measure of our lives! Which parent would turn down a generous offer of a little more time in their day?

Not Myra. Single mom. Immigrant. Hobbyist painter.

Myra unexpectedly finds the gift of time in an ordinary-looking mirror that cost her ten bucks. She steps into it for a much needed mid-day snooze when her little boy, Arjun, is away at school. She steps out to find that no time has lapsed in the real world in the meantime.

That additional time to rest and recover makes her a much better parent, she finds. And she is grateful for it.

Until Arjun stumbles into the mirror one day, leaving Myra

with no choice but to figure out with great urgency what price the mirror will extract from her for its gift of time.

Because sometimes, in life and in magic, there is no such thing as a free gift.

BEFORE WE BEGIN

Dear Reader,

Motherhood, or even parenting in general, is one of those life experiences that are almost universal yet remarkably unique to each one of us.

Everyone's parenting journey is vastly different. What works for one parent/family may simply not work for another.

My own journey has been a mix of unimaginable joys and unbelievable anxieties and everything else in between these two extremes.

During those dark moments, I turned to writing as a salve. I couldn't bring myself to speak aloud the fears I had for my child. Already wracked with anxiety and a deep sense of wrongness for even having those fears in the first place, I was terrified that putting them in written or spoken form—by journalling or talking about them to someone—might just make them come true.

Instead, I couched them in the guise of speculative fiction to render them more palatable, more surmountable, and as a reminder that in those moments my fears were exactly that—fiction!

It's for this very reason that I crafted the short story collection, *Your Mother's Nightmares*, a few months ago. *The Gift Of Time* is a short story from that six-tale collection.

If you're a parent, my hope is that in these pages, you too will find the words for the darkness you already know so intimately and grapple with every single day, and emerge into the light on the other side, feeling seen and sane and safe in the knowledge that you are doing the best you can and that is more than enough.

~ Anitha Krishnan
Burlington, Ontario,
Tuesday, 25 June 2024

THE GIFT OF TIME

1

The mirror had cost only ten dollars. Ten bucks for a full-length mirror. That itself should have been a dead giveaway. The first indicator that it was something someone wanted to be rid of.

Myra had inspected it thoroughly at the store. Its back was made of thin cardboard. The front had been wrapped in a milky plastic sheet, which had blurred her reflection.

It had a narrow white frame, certainly not made of wood. What it was made of, she couldn't tell. Something lightweight. She had been able to tuck it under one arm and walk out of the store to her car, guiding the shopping cart in front with her other hand while Arjun, her four-year-old, had pushed it.

All the other mirrors in the aisle had cost at least ten times as much. She hadn't given them a second glance. This one had been a fortuitous steal. She'd have been a fool to not buy it. Besides, she could always return it if it turned out to be one of those fun house mirrors that twisted you into ghoulish shapes.

Putting up the mirror on the wall beside the window in

their sole bedroom had proven to be yet another unexpectedly easy task. Two holes drilled into the wall. Two nails hammered into them. And up the mirror had gone.

There. Now she wouldn't have to prop her little boy up on the edge of the washbasin every time he wished to see himself from head to toe.

But the funny thing was that Arjun had not cared much for the mirror in their bedroom after it had gone up. That should have been the second sign that something was amiss.

Arjun had been genuinely excited at the store. He was the one who had pointed out the mirror to Myra in the first place, reminding her of a long-ago promise she had made to furnish the bedroom with a mirror.

Something that would ensure he never forgot how beautiful he was. Something that would remind her too, over and over again, how beautiful she was.

But once the plastic had been peeled away and the mirror had been nailed to the wall, Arjun behaved as if the damned thing didn't exist. Not a peek into it. Not even a sideways glance.

Even though the mirror reflected his beautiful self in the truest way possible. No distortions in shape or shade. Which had been a pleasant surprise, considering how cheap it had been.

But it wasn't until two days later that Myra caught a glimpse of what the mirror could actually do.

2

*I*t was Thursday night, and she was exhausted. Arjun had slept poorly this past week, waking Myra several times during the night. For water. He was thirsty. Or to push away the blanket. It was too hot. Or to ask for a blanket again. It was too cold.

After each interruption to the night, the child promptly drifted back into deep sleep, but Myra remained awake. Her body was overwhelmingly tired but her mind, once aroused, couldn't settle itself back into slumber.

When she closed her eyes, the sounds of the night amplified around her. The incessant ticking of the two-dollar clock from IKEA. The whisper of Arjun's breathing.

That was when she first heard it.

A soft fluttery sound. A gentle *rat-a-tat-tat-tat*. Interspersed with purrs. It seemed to come from the blinds on the window.

Myra lay in the dark, listening to it, wondering if it would let up.

It didn't.

A brief pause, here and there.

And then it resumed.

She reached for the bedside lamp and switched it on. The sound ceased.

She switched the lamp off and sank back into the mattress. Within a moment, the sound resumed.

Rat-a-tat-tat-tat. Rat-a-tat-tat-tat. A gentle clicking. Then *purrrr, purrrr.*

She switched the lamp on again and, like before, the sound ceased instantly in response. Night insects, perhaps. A moth on the window. Spiders mating.

She glanced at the clock on the wall. Two o'clock. Shen turned the lamp off and slumped back into bed, dreading the imminent arrival of a new day.

Arjun would be awake by five in the morning. Five-thirty at most. And Myra would have to drag herself through yet another day, nursing a nasty headache from lack of sleep, high on caffeine, and prone to irritation. The mere thought made her want to cry.

Tears filled her eyes like shiny things in the dark, obfuscating her view of the night beyond. She rubbed them away with the heels of her palms. Which is why she didn't see the strange light creep in and light up the room in a dim glow. When she opened her eyes, the room shimmered with muted light.

Myra had seen that light before. Every morning at six-thirty when the neighbour pulled their car out of their driveway. Light from the vehicle's headlamps spilled into the bedroom through the nearly closed slats and around the edges of the window blinds, swept through every inch of darkness, and probed every corner to tease out everything that wanted to remain hidden in the shadows.

Another sleepless soul, Myra thought sadly. It was only a momentary glow though. One that moved through the expanse of the room for a couple of moments, casting a slatted dance of light and shadow, and left just as quickly as it had come.

But this glow did not move. It stayed, as if it had come from within the room. It flickered on occasion, like a candle flame wobbling on its wick.

Myra looked towards the window, and realized the light was not coming through it. It was coming from the mirror beside the window.

It took her a few more moments to comprehend the thought that had just formed in her mind.

The light came from the mirror. Not the window.

From the other side of the mirror. Not from the other side of the window.

Both were surfaces of glass. One was transparent. The other was reflective.

One could let light through. The other couldn't. At least, it shouldn't.

Later, Myra would wonder why she hadn't felt afraid for herself, or for Arjun, at the first sight of light pouring inexplicably out of a mirror.

Later, she would tell herself that she had always known there was something unusual about the mirror, something a little off, for who in their right mind would sell a full-length mirror, with an almost-rare capacity for perfect reflection, for only ten dollars?

Or maybe, she'd rationalize later, she had read so many

picture books to Arjun in his four years of life on earth that very few things took her by surprise anymore. She had seen it all.

Flying cars. Talking owls. Holes dug through the centre of the earth and beyond. Dogs blasted off into space. Dinosaurs ferrying children to school. Donkeys wearing underpants on their heads.

After all that, a glowing mirror could hardly rattle her.

That night, she was merely inquisitive. Curious, she rolled out of bed, walked up to the mirror, and peered into it from the side. Only her craning face peered back at her. Bright and clear.

It took her a few moments to comprehend she was seeing something she shouldn't have been able to.

The room was dark, save for that dim glow. To any outside observer, she'd be nothing more than a silhouette. A deeper darkness carved out of night-space. Only the whites of her eyes should have been visible. This is what her mirror should have shown her too.

Instead, her mirror-self glowed. Her mirror-room shone a little, as if lit up from within, sharing some of its own light, no matter how feeble, with the rest of the world. A gleam in the dark. A glow-worm.

Cool, Myra thought. It didn't occur to her then that this was unusual behaviour for a mirror in real life.

She straightened up and positioned herself directly in front of the mirror. So did her reflection. Without warning, tiny points of light sparkled and pricked and shimmered in the mirror all around her reflection.

She reached out a hand and pressed it on the mirror, half-hoping it would give way and she'd go tumbling into a Narnia that had somehow opened its doors only for her.

Nothing happened.

The glass was as solid and unyielding as the wall beside it.

Disappointed, she peeled herself away from the mirror and tucked herself into bed once again. She turned to her side and gently ran her fingers through her child's hair. He liked to wear it long.

Tears rolled down her cheeks. More than four years had passed since Arjun's birth, yet Myra found herself breaking into unexpected tears more often than not.

Her baby was growing up too fast. Myra wanted to stop time in any which way possible, bring it to a screeching halt, the rest of the world be damned, for all she wanted was to trap herself and her child in this moment of innocence, in this moment of early childhood where magic and wonder prevailed. But time was running past relentlessly, as if it were desperate to get away from the here and now, as if it were in a real hurry to go someplace else, become something else.

Also, she needed to sleep. The tears spilled readily when she had been neglecting her own self for too long. She hadn't slept well in days. She had been subsisting on leftovers and snacks, even though she heaped Arjun's plate and lunchbox with fresh fruits and rainbow-coloured meals.

The unremarkable ordinariness of the mirror was the last straw. She should have known better than to seek magic in a cheap mirror.

Even the whole wide world, with its collective wisdom on living and parenting, often seemed so devoid of beauty and magic. How could a mere piece of glass be any different?

3

For two nights, Myra made a conscious effort to be in bed by half-past eight, so she could sleep when Arjun slept and wake up alongside him at five the next morning.

This meant she couldn't catch the latest episode of *Murdoch Mysteries* right when it aired on CBC TV. Eight o'clock on Monday nights. That would have to wait until Saturday afternoon to coincide with Arjun's designated weekly TV time.

Netflix binges had long become an alien concept to her. When she spent four or five hours at night enjoying episode after episode of *Bridgerton* and then made do with barely two or three hours of sleep, she typically spent the next day being an irate mother, snapping at her four-year-old when he insisted on wearing his socks all by himself, even if it meant he'd be late for school.

She didn't want to be an angry mother like the one she'd had. She wanted to be a good mother, an epitome of calm, a personification of gentle grace, a parent who role-modelled emotional maturity, and not emotional distress, to her child.

And for the most part, she managed to pull it off. So long as she slept well, ate well, made small but steady progress on the collection of paintings she had begun working on two months ago, she felt fulfilled.

From that well of contentment sprung unconditional love for her and for Arjun, a child who was a natural delight. She wanted to be a safe place for him to express himself, his entire range of emotions and thoughts.

When she was present and attentive to his needs and her own, she was a great mother, a parent who adored her child, who found everything about this little human utterly fascinating.

The only trouble was it was all boring as hell. The entire ordinary, predictable routine.

Waking up with Arjun. Enjoying a fun morning routine of breakfast and packing lunch and getting ready for school. Dropping him off.

Coming back home, now serene and peaceful, the entire space stirring her creativity. Losing herself for a few hours in her artwork. The act of creation filling her up in a way even motherhood could not.

Taking some time in the afternoon to enjoy a cup of tea. Preparing dinner.

Picking up Arjun. Enjoying the drive back home, enchanted with all his tales of a busy day at school.

Relishing dinnertime with him. Cleaning up. Bathing her child. Reading to him. Realizing he has fallen asleep mid-reading, head on her chest.

Peeling herself away from under him. Shifting him to a more comfortable position. Pulling the blanket up to his chin.

Gazing at his innocent face, watching the subtle rise and fall of his blanket in rhythm with the movement of his chest under it. Whispering to her sleeping child how grateful she was to have him in her life. Acknowledging what a privilege it was.

Realizing how perfect her life had become, how easy it had been to make her life perfect.

Conceding that when she was happy, Arjun was happy too, safe in the knowledge that his home, his haven was not under any threat of mutating out of its current comfortable form anytime soon.

Castigating herself, out of habit, for not being able to hold on to this perfection, for always letting it slip away just as easily as it made its way back into her life.

Stepping into the shower or running a warm bath for herself. Meditating for twenty minutes right after. Tucking herself into bed right next to Arjun. Falling asleep in time to ensure a good eight hours or more of uninterrupted rest.

Waking up just a few minutes before her little one did. Beginning the day by gifting herself the space and time to prepare. Prepare to surrender, prepare to bend like water and flow, no matter what the day presented to them.

4

Typically, she was able to keep up this routine for three days, or four at most. Then something would pat her on the back and tell her, "Good job! You've earned your rest now. You deserve a break."

And then she'd be right back on Netflix, prowling through the endless web of trailers in the hour right before she'd have to go and pick Arjun up from school, forsaking her cup of afternoon tea and deciding between leftovers and takeout for dinner, salivating at the sight of all those other worlds, beckoning to her, their doorways opening wide, luring her inside, so she could lose herself and escape from the reality that her life had become, a reality that felt like it would never change.

The reality of routine, of prediction, of monotony. Of utter, unimaginable sameness.

The sky steeped in the same, unchanging blue. Leaf-buds swelling obscenely like hard nipples on springtime branches. Tulips and daffodils blooming on the lawns of neighbours who had too much time on their hands and too little imagination in their heads.

It was all maddeningly mediocre. Like a magic trick she had seen so often it had lost all its charm even though she still hadn't figured out how it all worked. Surely, she deserved a break.

And that would be the night everything would come crashing down again.

A late-night Netflix binge. Falling asleep at three. Waking up at five. Spending the day like a bear with a sore head. Brushing away her four-year-old every time he asked her to play with him. Pain exploding through her head.

Arjun putting up a brave front at first. Arjun eventually beginning to whine, surely sensing something amiss in her, in their home, something that had been so perfect only last evening, something that had disappeared overnight, and who knew if it will ever come back again.

Guilt coursing through her veins, terror of all the anxiety she was filling him up with, shame for all the parenting failures she was committing now, mistakes that would surely come back to haunt her in the years to come.

Wondering how it had all come to this. Cursing herself for not being able to do the simple things. Eating. Conversing. Chilling out.

Switching on *Paw Patrol* on the TV to keep her little one occupied, to keep him away from her. Promising herself she'd resume her routine of going to bed no later than half-past eight tonight.

Feeling infuriated that she couldn't even allow herself a sliver of entertainment.

Feeling mad at her child for turning her world upside down.

Feeling incensed by the knowledge that Nick, her ex-husband, now blessedly child-free, was soaking up the sunshine in Hawaii with his latest girlfriend.

Feeling irate at her parents whom she had left behind in another continent for the sake of a man who had left *her* behind in turn, unwilling to be saddled with a child, whose grandparents were loathe to travel halfway across the world to help care for their only grandchild.

Feeling terrified that after all her attempts to ensure otherwise, she was indeed turning into her own mother.

Feeling abandoned by society and the government and the institution of marriage, all abstract concepts that made promises they never kept.

Wishing this day would end right now.

Wishing she could simply crawl back under the covers and sleep. Sleep, sleep, and sleep until eternity.

5

*A*n offering.

The idea came to Myra a few days later when Arjun said he'd like to visit a temple to see what God was all about (an idea planted into his head by his faraway grandparents), and she had insisted on first purchasing fresh flowers and fruits to offer to the deities. A customary practice she did not believe in but had felt obliged to pass on knowledge of to her son, for him to decide whether or not it was worth following.

The offering had to be of value, she decided, not necessarily financial but something that bore some significance to her. A price that was immeasurable.

She chose one of her early paintings. A watercolour she had conjured to life for pleasure, for fun, before years of education and expert advice had sullied her creativity and rendered her art predictable, jaded.

Now she was unlearning what she had learnt. Trying to regain the spontaneity she had lost, keenly aware of the irony inherent in such an endeavour.

She hadn't even framed her work, refusing to confine it any more than the paper itself did, the archival paper on which she had painted a brook, tumbling blithely towards an unseen destination, meandering through a green meadow in the shade of summertime trees, birds and butterflies darting about, drawing streaks of colours in the air around them, white clouds adrift, breaking up the sameness of the blue sky, and the sun generously warm but not too hot on this beautiful day.

Blue skies and white clouds. For as long as she could remember, they had been undeniable images of happiness. The sight of fluffy white clouds drifting in a blue sky filled her heart with an inexplicable lightness, as if she too could fly, for somehow the sight of them had helped her shed the onus she had been carrying, the burden of living.

Or maybe that had been the picture of happiness planted in her head by Enid Blyton. The summertime escapades of the *Famous Five* had become Myra's own in her childhood.

She used to imagine herself as George, fierce and courageous, diving headlong into the most dangerous of adventures, refusing to be limited by gender stereotyping.

But look at Myra now! Keeping house like Anne. Sweet, domestic Anne.

That realization had stolen her love for blue skies and white clouds. The sight of them no longer bewitched her.

Clutching her painting in her hands, she stood in front of the mirror. It was early afternoon. Half-past one. Sunlight streamed into the bedroom through the south-facing window adjacent to the mirror. A light lunch and two espressos had done little to keep exhaustion at bay. Drowsiness clung to her as if it had nowhere else to go.

But she couldn't afford the luxury of sleep now. In less than two hours, she'd need to pick Arjun up from school. Several mothers on the internet swore by power naps. But Myra worried that if she were to close her eyes now, she'd be dead to the world for days.

Her mirror-self smiled and held out her hand. Myra presented her painting to the mirror, brushing it lightly against the surface of the glass. At the lightest touch, her painting was whisked into the mirror and out of sight.

In an explosion of soundless light, the mirror opened itself to her, its glow billowing out and engulfing her until she stepped forward and entered the world behind the mirror, without quite seeing where it began and where her own room ended.

Sprawling meadows unfurled at her feet and met a lazy blue sky at the horizon. A brook burbled beside where she stood. A cardinal sang from somewhere above her, coaxing new leaves to spring forth. The fragrance of unnamed wildflowers tickled her nose, lingering briefly before disappearing into the aether once more.

Soft grass kissed her bare feet as she took one step, then another, breathing in the dewy scent of the clean air around her.

She came upon a picnic mat, held in place by stones on three corners while the fourth corner flapped occasionally in the cool breeze. She sank into the centre of the mat and lay down on her back. The sun was a little behind her, out of sight, but her limbs relaxed in his generous warmth.

She closed her eyes and succumbed to sleep.

6

*M*yra awoke slowly. She stirred to the scents and sounds around her, reluctant to open her eyes. The cardinal whistled sweetly. A warm breeze soothed her body. The stream gurgled like a baby.

It reminded her of Arjun, when he was a baby, so content to remain in her arms, yet to rise to the bait of the world outside.

Mumma! A distant shout jarred her out of her reverie.

Arjun! She opened her eyes and sat up so quickly she almost pulled a muscle in her back. Her child was nowhere to be seen.

Was he still at school? She had no idea how long she had been asleep for. A heavy sense of dread squeezed her heart and made her gasp. She looked around. The sun still shone behind her, almost exactly where it had been when she had fallen asleep. Perhaps she had had only a power nap after all?

Then the next thought nagged her. How was she to get back to her world? She looked up the way she had come, and sure enough, the air in the distance shimmered like a mirage. A sheer curtain fluttering in the wind. A veil between worlds.

She jumped up and hurtled towards it, heart in mouth, afraid it would disappear before she could reach it.

But it didn't. It opened up as she approached it. A great chasm. A vast nothingness.

She leapt into it and tumbled onto the floor in their bedroom. Her back twinged once more. Argh! She was getting too old for these antics.

She first sought the clock on the wall. Half-past one. Half-past one? She shook her head, frantic. Had the clock stopped working? But no, the second hand was still spinning and ticking.

The room swam around her. She put a hand to her head as if she needed to hold it in place, lest it should fall down and roll away from her body, so utterly discombobulated was she.

The second hand swept past the number twelve. The minute hand lurched forward. A strangled cry of relief, of hope, escaped Myra's lips.

She looked into the mirror, and there was her mirror-self, smiling at her, a calm witness to Myra's confusion, a source of assurance that whatever had transpired this afternoon, no harm had been done.

With a renewed burst of energy in her limbs, Myra changed into a pair of jeans and a button-down shirt, grabbed her phone and purse and keys, and dashed out the door like a woman possessed.

The springtime sun in her world was still high up in the sky, she noticed without quite registering the fact. It was only when she pulled into the parking lot of Arjun's school that she paused to think for a moment.

Several cars were parked in the sprawling lot. Teachers' cars. On the basketball court beyond the school building, a group of older children played under the supervision of a grown-up. A coach, from the looks of it.

A few more groups of children were playing in different parts of the grassy grounds that unfurled behind the main school building. She squinted her eyes to see if Arjun was among them, but the children were too far away for her to identify him or his classmates.

She scrutinized the school building. Windows had been thrown open in some of the classes. An invitation to the warm breeze.

Myra rolled down the car window, and the unmistakable buzz of a busy day at school thrummed the air around her. Indecipherable shouts. An occasional whistle, like that of a referee's. The general hum of activity and sound that busy children seemed to emanate all the time, no matter what they were up to, except perhaps when they fell asleep.

She picked up her phone, her hands shaking with relief and confusion. It was nearly two in the afternoon. Arjun's school wouldn't draw to a close for at least another hour and a half. Surely, he must be inside too. But she had to make sure.

When one of the admin assistants at the school answered her call, Myra said, "Hi, this is Ms. Raman. My child, Arjun, is in JK."

"Of course, Ms. Raman, what can I do for you?" The lady pronounced it as 'ramen'.

Myra hadn't known what she'd say but the pretext now came to her glibly, as if it had been sitting on the tip of her tongue all along, merely waiting for her permission to roll off.

"Arjun was a little upset this morning at drop-off," she

explained. "He hasn't been sleeping well these past few nights. I had promised to swing by at around two to see if he was doing OK or if he'd like to come back home early today."

"Sure, I'll take a look for you."

Myra didn't have to wait long.

"Nothing to worry about, Ms. Raman. He's playing with his friends now. It's free play time for them and their class teacher has taken them outdoors. She says he's had a great day so far. Would you still like to pick him up now?"

Relief flooded Myra's body. "That's OK. I'll come back at the usual pick-up time. Thank you for checking."

She had more than an hour to spare. She drove to the nearest Starbucks, grabbed a tall hazelnut latte, and made her way down to the beach, a fifteen-minute drive away from Arjun's school.

And there she sat on the sand, soft and grainy now, not hard and clumpy like it had been a fortnight ago when the city had still been in the grip of one of the coldest winters on record. The great lake was placid. Small waves of water gently brushed against the shore and retreated without fuss.

And there she sat and thought and thought about the mirror, that cheap ten-dollar purchase, that had somehow led her into a different world where time stood still.

7

_G_rowing up, Myra had been sensible and lucky enough to steer clear of the trap of addiction.

But now, as a single parent, she had been so deprived of sleep for so long she thought she'd give anything, anything barring her life and that of her only child, to get some sleep.

Deep, uninterrupted sleep. More precisely, some _time_ to sleep well.

When Arjun was away at school, there were so many things she had to attend to that sleep was a luxury she could ill afford in his absence.

But now the mirror had solved this conundrum for her. Since that fateful afternoon, she had taken to stepping daily into the mirror-world, still a panorama of meadows and brook and blue sky and white clouds, and had fallen into deep sleep easily, assuredly.

Each time, she had woken up gently, slowly, and had walked through that crevice in space back into their bedroom to find that time in the real world had held its breath, waiting patiently for her to return, before it could resume its forward march once again.

It was such a perfect arrangement that she tried as hard as she could to keep the doubts at bay. They'd come eventually, she knew that for a fact. But for now, she tried to take things slowly, keep them simple.

She set a few ground rules for herself.

First, she would use the mirror only when she was alone at home.

Typically, in the afternoon hours that stretched languidly between lunch hour and pick-up time. That was when she felt most drowsy. Slumber then became an extravagant treat, rendered all the more enjoyable and rejuvenating when it followed an entire morning dedicated to her art.

Second, she would not make Arjun privy to the mirror's magic.

She still didn't know enough about the mirror and its workings to introduce an impressionable child to its enigma. Perhaps, some day when he was old enough, some day when he had children of his own and yearned for restful sleep, she would pass on the mirror to him like a family heirloom. For now, it was best he remained in the dark. He showed the mirror so little interest anyway she had no intentions of drawing his attention back to it.

Third, she would not enter the mirror at night.

For one thing, that would be in violation of her first rule. She was never alone at home at night-time. Arjun was in bed every night, and even if slipping into the mirror meant she'd be back before another moment had passed in the real world, it was a risk not worth taking. The possibility, no matter how slight, that Arjun might wake up in the dark of the night, find himself alone, and call out to his mother only to realize she had gone missing, was so terrifying that she had no intentions of ever tempting fate in this matter.

For another, she knew from a lifetime of living that the world at night was vastly different than at daytime. The creatures that came out at night never revealed themselves in the light of the day. Nature must have had her reasons for keeping apart the lives of diurnal and nocturnal creatures. Unless Myra could determine if the mirror-world too separated night and day, she was content with all that it offered her. Eternal sunshine to sleep in as the rest of the world came to a halt.

The most gratifying outcome of this development was that she had become the perfect mom. Well-rested, she was calm and collected every moment of the day she spent with Arjun.

He was already such a sweet child. On those rare occasions when impulse took over and he kicked his shoes away, frustrated at not being able to tie his own laces, or threw his coat down, unable to put it up on a hanger, or sat on the floor and cried for half an hour, bogged down by a long day of mental stimulation and physical exertion at school, Myra became the kind of parent every child needed.

Graceful under pressure. Calm in the face of her child's storm. Role-modelling empathy and equanimity in the most difficult of situations.

Not even feeling the urge to shush her child or rush him through his feelings or wishing he'd stop crying. No. None of those primal urges that drive parents crazy because what they want is the impossible—for their child to never have to encounter pain.

Instead, she became the parent she had always wanted to

be, and better still, she found that now she could be this parent all the time. This Zen parent, who'd never again turn into an angry, yelling mumzilla, the default state of most sleep-deprived caregivers, the state that she too lapsed into occasionally back in the day, before the mirror had graced her bedroom wall.

Even now, the memory of her lapses of composure wrecked her with guilt. After every outburst, when sanity was eventually restored, she worried that these lapses alone would cost her child much, much more than he'd gain in emotional health by her peaceful parenting practice at all other times.

She shook her head to brush that thought away. Why dwell on a past that would never repeat itself? She had found a cure to sleep deprivation.

And even the phantom baby cries she had been hearing since the day Arjun was born, like a horrible case of tinnitus, had disappeared. Whoever knew that just the right amount of sleep and rest could make a world of difference in their lives?

The fourth ground rule she set was this: she must attempt to determine the price she has to pay for this magic.

It was not a rule per se, but Myra had never been one to sponge off others, let alone a magic mirror. So far, the mirror had only been giving her the gift of time to do with as she pleased. She always chose to sleep. She had given the mirror only her cherished painting, which had come to life in this hidden world. The gift she had given had been imbued with magic and gifted back to her again.

The more she thought about it, the more uncomfortable she grew, although not enough to quit stepping into the mirror for her early afternoon naps. Like a smoker who derived guilty pleasure from each drag, each puff, worrying on one hand when the death knell would sound but opting for instant gratification in lieu of longevity and good health, which even abstinence could never truly guarantee.

Myra too had grown accustomed and addicted to those bonus hours of sleep. She could no longer imagine getting through a day without them.

This was especially true on weekends and on school holidays when Arjun was at home all day. Unless he was away at camp or at a friend's place, Myra was compelled to wait for the next opportunity to slip into the mirror without being missed or noticed.

But knowing there was an end to this wait, seeing the flicker of light at the end of the tunnel was all the impetus she needed to keep going.

But she needed to know what she'd be asked to forfeit when the time came. The more she enjoyed this precious gift of time, the more she worried she might be asked to pay an inconceivable price for it.

8

*A*rjun wanted to become Aria when he was six.

It all began when his cousins crossed the pond to visit them that summer. His maternal uncle, aunt, and cousins —seven-year-old Priya and eleven-year-old Sunny—had come and stayed with them for a fortnight.

What a ball they'd all had! Mornings at the beach. Afternoons in the backyard. Evenings at playgrounds in the neighbourhood. Nights spent falling asleep gazing at stars in the backyard, although every morning they somehow woke up in the comfortable bed in the bedroom Arjun still shared with his mother, co-sleeping the only form of sleeping he had ever known since he was born.

But what struck him most about their visit was Priya's wonderful, colourful attire. Frocks and skirts, frilly tops and sporty tights, hairbands and ribbons. She was a rainbow, so many and varied and vivid were the colours she wore.

For some reason, Arjun had had the sense to wait until his cousins had gone back across the pond to approach his mother with the desire that had been burning in his little six-year-old heart. "Can I wear a skirt, please?"

Myra, that perfect mother, that all-accepting parent whose only mission in life was to ensure she stayed out of her son's way, hugged him in response and said, "Why, of course, sweetie!"

The first frock she bought for him was a pink-and-orange affair, one small step towards change. Arjun loved it.

He first wore it on a day in late-August summer, when the sun was still high in the sky and the bedroom, with its south-facing windows, was flooded with bright light. He wore it and twirled in front of the mirror, delighted with the swish and the swirl of the fabric, the way the colours danced in his reflection.

And his mirror-self smiled at him. He paused mid-twirl, but his mirror-self continued to whirl.

Eyes wide with curiosity, he stepped closer to the mirror. His mirror-self paused in his dance, then moved closer to him too.

Arjun pressed a hand on the mirror. His mirror-self did too.

The glass shivered and shimmered, like ripples on the face of a lake.

Arjun's hand passed through the glass, now a soft, grey nothingness. Another hand clasped his. Certainly, his mirror-self's.

Without a moment's hesitation, he slipped through.

9

*M*yra was waiting for the coffee machine to fill her cup when, for the briefest of moments, the world around her came crashing to a standstill.

Only for a moment. Not even.

An insignificant pause in the earth's revolution around the sun. As if the unstoppable planet had encountered a little bump in its orbit. Not enough to throw it off course, but enough to cause a slight judder.

Even the coffee pouring out of the machine had seemed to pause in its downward flow.

Myra blinked. Her mouth stretched into an involuntary yawn. This was the longest she had gone without disappearing into the mirror for her daily fix of slumber. Her brother and his family had left only a week ago, and she missed them dearly. As did Arjun. Or Aria now. He couldn't decide. The familiarity of his old self played tug-of-war with the novelty of his new self. The possibility that he could become someone else altogether was still an exhilaratingly new idea.

She tried to remain objective about his explorations. But in her heart of hearts, she hoped it was only a passing phase. A sudden interest in something new, something unfamiliar, for she herself often dressed in trousers and tops.

Deep down, she was utterly terrified. The world was still too insecure to tolerate any display of authenticity that was contrary to its standards.

And Arjun was such a sweet boy. He had not a sliver of aggression in him. So many girls these days were way more aggressive than her sweet boy.

That was the trouble with today's world. For aeons, it had upheld the stereotypes of docile girls and aggressive boys. People had been terrified of loud girls and ashamed of sensitive boys.

And now loud girls were celebrated whereas sensitive boys, already too quiet to begin with, have grown even quieter, unsure of their place in this world where the one who shouts the loudest for the longest is heard and all other voices are drowned in the din.

Today's world was a terrifying place for tender boys, even if nothing else about their appearance or attire or attitudes drew unwarranted flak.

A desire to spend the afternoon playing board games with Arjun tugged at her heart.

Off late, he had taken to spending more and more time by himself. She was loathe to disturb him when he was so engrossed in his life. Reading. Drawing. Practising chords on his synth. Thinking. Dreaming. Watching clouds drift and butterflies flit. Sashaying about in his frock (she ought to buy him more dresses and skirts) and admiring himself in the mirror.

The mirror!

Coffee forgotten, she ran up the stairs two at a time into their bedroom and dashed through the open door. Arjun was sitting on the bed, dressed in his pink and orange frock, looking out the window. He turned to her and smiled.

"Are you OK?" Myra asked, plonking herself beside him and trying to steady her breath.

"You won't believe what just happened."

"What happened?"

"I met Aria." He grinned.

"Aria?"

"Yes." He nodded.

"Aria, as in yourself?"

Another nod.

"I don't understand," Myra said.

"In the mirror," he explained, pointing towards the white-framed, cheap mirror that hung on the wall innocently.

Heart in throat, Myra swallowed and said, "Your reflection, you mean?"

"Hmm, yeah," Arjun said, knitting his eyebrows, the way he usually did when taking his time to choose the right words to say. Myra wished he'd hurry up and tell her what he had seen in the mirror, what the mirror had shown him. "But she's also her own person. And she took me to her home."

"Her home?" Myra tried to hold her voice steady.

"Yeah. Where she lives. Inside the mirror."

hat night, Myra broke her first and third rules in a desperate attempt to follow the fourth. The mirror had laid bare its secrets to Arjun. Consequently, the second rule, that her sweet, tender boy shall not be made privy to its magic, was irreparably broken.

She stood in front of the mirror, uttering a silent prayer that she'd meet someone who would explain to her the magic of the mirror.

When the mirror shimmered and sparkled, she stepped into its glow, leaving behind Arjun, alone and fast asleep in their bedroom in the middle of the night.

She hadn't expected to step into the noontime meadow of her painting, yet the darkness of the world behind the mirror unnerved her quite a bit. Strange, unfriendly creatures lurked in the dark, her mother had often told her, not referring to the paranormal kind but the very real human type.

As her eyes grew accustomed to the darkness, her own bedroom appeared as a recognizable pattern of silhouettes against the pale light of the night. Everything on this side of the mirror was identical to that on the other side, except for Arjun. Her child was not here. Just as surely as she was not in her bedroom, the real one.

But someone else was. A shadow peeled itself away from the far darkness and glided towards her. Before it approached her, it drifted to the wall on the other side of the bed. With a click of a switch, the room in the mirror was flooded with light.

Myra instinctively squeezed her eyes shut in response to the unexpected explosion of light, then blinked a few times until it no longer stung.

And then she saw her. Herself. Her mirror-self. Smiling. And then the smile stretched into a yawn.

"Sorry," her mirror-self said, mid-yawn. She even sounded like Myra. Perhaps, a little more elegant.

Her pyjamas were identical to those of Myra's. The top featuring a penguin wearing a scarf and a caption that read, "Baby, it's cold outside!" and capri pants with rows of penguins sporting scarfs of different colours.

On her mirror-self, the pyjamas appeared tailor-made. Her hair was tousled but somehow she managed to pull off the messy look. It came across as chic on her. As far as Myra's messy hair was concerned, even a bird's nest would have appeared far tidier in comparison.

Every time Myra looked into the mirror for the sole purpose of appraising her appearance, she had been dissatisfied. And now, encountering her mirror-self in this mirror-world, Myra felt even dowdier than ever before.

"It's not your fault," her mirror-self said. "That's what mirrors do."

"What do mirrors do?"

"They take your beauty and stash it away, until you stop looking into them to understand how beautiful you truly are."

Myra mulled over this revelation. It made sense to her but also didn't. Like a koan. A puzzling way to ignite a realization, a spark of enlightenment.

Her mirror-self sat on the bed and beckoned to Myra to join her. Myra sat on the edge of the bed, feeling like an intruder in her own bedroom. Even her mirror-self was a distinct entity.

Her reflection bore a softness that Myra often found lacking in her own self. A nurturing gentleness. As if her mirror-self was someone who could be a very good friend to Myra.

Had the mirror taken that too from her? Or had Myra turned all her care and affection outwards, towards Arjun, sparing nothing for her own self?

"Is that the price I pay for the gift of time this mirror gives me?" Myra asked.

Her mirror-shelf shook her head. "No, that is merely the price you pay for looking into a mirror. Any mirror, not this one alone."

"That's quite a hefty price to pay for seeking one's own beauty in a mirror."

"You could look at it that way, I suppose."

"I wonder then, what price you'll make me pay for all the times I've stepped into the mirror and fallen asleep in this world."

Her mirror-self smiled. "Not me. I don't ask for anything. I am nothing more than who you are. It is the mirror that sets the rules and we abide by them."

"What are these rules? Please tell me. I must know."

"You are worried for Arjun," her mirror-self said.

Myra nodded. "I'm always worried for him," she said before she could stop herself. She was admitting, for the first time in her life, to another adult how anxiety had become her default state when it came to all matters pertaining to Arjun. "And if I'm not aware, that anxiety soars out of control and morphs into anger. Which is why I find it is so crucial for me to sleep well. To rest and heal. Leave behind one day fully before entering another."

Her mirror-self understood. "The first time you came here, you slept for half a day," she said. "Twelve hours in one go."

Myra laughed.

"Off late, you've settled to a fairly consistent eight or nine hours," her mirror-self added.

"How is it that all that time passes in this world, but when I go back to the real world, not a moment has gone by without me?"

"Like beauty, time is another element that seeps from your world into ours."

It became quite clear to Myra what this statement of fact implied. "Will that leave me with less time in the real world?"

"Yes," her mirror-self said. "The time that you gain in this world, you pay for it with time from your own life in the real world."

"How?"

"For every hour that you spend here, you give up several times as many hours of your lifetime in the real world."

"But I haven't lost any time in the real world," Myra said.

"Not yet. Because those hours are culled from the end of your life."

Realization hit Myra like a slap in the face. "Say I was

originally destined to die when I turn eighty years old. But now, because of my meanderings into this mirror-world, I may die at the age of seventy?"

Her mirror-self nodded. "I wouldn't put a precise number to it. Because no one ever knows when they'll die. But you will die sooner than you were fated to. That is the price you pay."

A heavy weight settled in Myra's heart. She put a hand on her chest and rubbed it. Words failed her.

"A mirror can only give back to you what you put into it," her mirror-self said. "Never an exact replica, but warped in some way."

11

A child of older parents, Myra had been only fifteen years old when her mother turned fifty and her father turned sixty-one.

The near-overnight decline in their health and zest for life had made Myra pray silently to whichever Gods deigned to listen that she wouldn't live a day past fifty. There was little joy in living, merely existing, without the energy and exuberance of youth, she had reasoned haughtily.

Now, having turned forty only a few months ago, Myra was as terrified of the prospect of death as Arjun had been at the age of four.

Now that she had a child, Myra no longer wanted to die at fifty. She wanted to live forever. Old enough to see Arjun grow up, marry, have babies of his own. One lifetime was not enough.

She wanted to spend countless lifetimes with her child, watch his life unfold, and hoard the knowledge of every single detail of his life, now and forevermore, just as how she had known everything about him ever since he was born—what his every coo or gurgle or cry implied, what he longed for, what hurt or scared him, and what made his heart sing.

Petrified, she started to do the math. How long had she spent in the mirror so far? How many weeks or months did all those hours add up to? How many months or years will be wrenched out of her life as a consequence?

How much longer of this life did she have? Twenty years? Ten? Will she die tomorrow? Will she die right now?

Forty-year-old single mother dies in sleep. Six-year-old son orphaned.

The captions flashed in the eye of her mind like a news ticker.

Like a prophecy. An omen. The thought terrified her. But rage quickly followed fear.

Furious with herself, Myra pushed away her blanket and marched out of the bedroom. She headed straight down to the kitchen and prepared a cup of coffee. It was three in the morning. Arjun would wake up in another two hours. And sleep was determinedly elusive.

As the coffee machine sputtered and hissed and spat out the near-black potion, Myra's frantic mind quietened. Setting aside her fearful extrapolation of the situation, she tried to recall what her mirror-self had said.

No one ever knows when they will die.

What if Myra would have lived past hundred but now she'd only live until she turned ninety? Or even eighty or seventy or sixty for that matter?

Wasn't she having a grand time with Arjun now? She shared such an easy-going, respectful bond with her child, surely a few years at the fag end of her life were worth forfeiting.

Look at her own parents now. Mother would turn seventy-five soon and Father was eighty-six years old. For all practical purposes, they were non-existent in her life. They had disowned her a decade ago when she had chosen to elope with Nick.

That she was marrying *out of caste* was deemed an act of sacrilege by her South Indian middle-class parents. She was also marrying *out of religion, out of skin colour, out of nationality,* sins from which there'd never be any redemption for her.

"You might as well marry a green alien from outer space!" her mother had shrieked.

Arjun's arrival had done little to mellow their anger, though they had condescended to chat with their only grandson on FaceTime every weekend. The sight of him sashaying about in a skirt would deal yet another blow to whatever pretence of a relationship with them she clung to.

She sipped her coffee, wishing for the first time in a long time she had a cigarette to steady her nerves. Not yet four in the morning. A little more than one hour to go before Arjun woke up and the long, long day ahead of them would begin. She was already beginning to feel resentful of his existence in her life.

No. No. No. That way lay madness all over again.

Perhaps she could drive to the nearest convenience store and buy some smokes. It would take no longer than seven minutes. But what if Arjun chose this particular morning to wake up earlier than usual only to find her gone? How would that damage and scar his psyche? Not to mention, the various child endangerment and protection laws she'd violate by this small, impulsive act.

She opened the main door and stepped out barefoot. A

blast of cold, dewy air brought her to her literal senses. Goosebumps prickled the skin on her arms. A robin trilled in the distance. The scent of clean, crisp air cleansed her lungs. The sky was a dark blue-purple, an indescribable shade of new beginnings.

She took a sip of her coffee and at once, its bitter taste was at odds with everything else around her. She stared into her mug and frowned at the beverage. A manmade concoction of substances that disrupted sleep patterns. Ever since she had been catching up on sleep in the mirror-world, her need for coffee in the real world had diminished.

Often, she reached for a cuppa out of unconscious habit, an addiction, the way a smoker lights up another stick without even thinking about it, his hands and lips automatically doing what they've learned to, what they've been trained to, despite the images of sickness and death plastered on the packets.

Come to think of it, smoking a cigarette to collect herself was hardly any different than disappearing into the mirror for a few hours of rest. The certainty of short-term pleasure was more alluring than the unpredictability of long-term safety.

It was all a crap shoot, anyway. No one ever knows when they will die. You could smoke a pack a day and live to a hundred or beyond. You could abstain from all the vices ever known to mankind yet nothing would stop an errant driver from knocking you down accidentally on your twentieth birthday.

Besides, her mirror-self had said there was no way to tell how many hours of her lifetime Myra would have to forfeit. What if for every hour she spent in the mirror, she only had to give up half an hour of her life? If there was no way to know, it all came down to what she believed, didn't it?

At least, this way she was a much better mom to Arjun and a much calmer person, kinder and gentler and more present with herself than she had ever been.

She turned back inside and poured out the rest of her coffee into the sink. Upstairs she went, quietly, and was relieved to find Arjun still fast asleep.

The sight of her sleeping child never failed to move her heart. The rise and fall of his chest with every breath, his six-year-old body lying spreadeagled, not a care in the world. For why should he worry? He had a mother whose love he was assured of.

Myra kissed him gently on his cheek, then tiptoed away from the bed and into the mirror.

Right now, it was time to sleep.

Ready for more fantasy short stories on the motherhood experience? Check out the collection, Your Mother's Nightmares: Six Troubling Tales, which includes five more twisted tales on the motherhood experience.

When you buy the collection directly from my store, please treat yourself to a 40% discount using the code YMN40.

Please note the code YMN40 is valid only for the short story collection — Your Mother's Nightmares: Six Troubling Tales — in ebook format when purchased directly from my PayHip store, Dream Pedlar Books.
Go to https://payhip.com/b/SfQvj to redeem your code!

ENJOYED THE GIFT OF TIME?

Thank you for reading *The Gift Of Time*!

If you loved the story, I hope you will consider writing a short review—even a simple line or two—on the site where you bought the book.

Publishing is still driven by word of mouth, and when you leave a review it helps other readers decide this is a story worth reading. Thank you for your help in spreading the word.

You can also sign up to my monthly newsletter for updates on new book releases as well as heartfelt reflections on writing, reading, parenting and living the creative life.

Monthly Missives from The Dream Pedlar
https://thedreampedlar.com/newsletter

AUTHOR'S NOTE

Dear Reader,

Time becomes such a precious commodity the instant a child arrives. It feels as though there's always so much to do and so little time to get it all done. Not to mention how we all crave for deep, uninterrupted sleep.

Being a parent then becomes an excellent exercise in shedding all that's not valuable to us and guarding space and time only for the handful of things we truly cherish.

For me, I only want to spend time on my child Dhruv (D), my husband Abhinav, and writing. I don't really have any hobbies, to be honest, and I don't much care for them, except reading, of course.

Off late, I've added healthy living to the mix, now that D has just turned eight and I do have the twin luxuries of time and lack of parental guilt to devote some time to working out and making healthier food choices than I used to.

Some elements in this story are true. We didn't have a full-length mirror at home, so whenever D wanted to look at himself from head to toe, we'd lift him up and prop him by the edge of the sink so he could take a look in the mirror above it.

We found a cheap $10 mirror at Canadian Tire one day, and put it up in D's room. One night I did see the strange lights and hear the clicking sounds in D's room, which went away every time I switched on the bedside lamp.

D also used to love pink and purple as his favourite colours. He used to sashay about in my tunics and enjoy wearing my jewelry. In his early days at school, he was a vocal supporter of 'anybody can like any colour, anybody can wear anything'.

As was wont to happen, the opinions of the world outside have slowly been making him doubt his choices.

When he started to question himself, I once happily showed him the pictures of the singer Harry Styles wearing a skirt. (Styles is a familiar name to D as we've heard his songs on the radio quite often. *As It Was. Adore You. Watermelon Sugar.*)

We've stood by D steadfastly, often reminding him that other's opinions of him are fleeting at best and do not really matter.

He is not always convinced, and I reckon this journey of going away and coming back to his true self is something he'll have to make over the course of his lifetime.

We can only keep reminding him how amazing he is and that we love him just the way he is. It's a lesson to be learnt over a lifetime, even for us grown-ups!

Thank you, dear Reader, for reading this far. I'd love to stay in touch with you. And I hope you'd like to stay connected with me too.

I send out a monthly newsletter on the last Sunday of

every month filled with heartfelt musings on the joys of writing, reading and living the creative life. Subscription is free.

You will be the first to hear of my forthcoming works. I also include updates on my writing life, book recommendations, free short fiction, and occasional surprises.

Thank you for staying with me this far. If you choose to accompany me further on this journey, I promise you a magical ride.

Climb aboard at https://thedreampedlar.com/newsletter!

~ Anitha Krishnan
Burlington, Ontario
Tuesday, 25 June 2024

MORE BOOKS BY ANITHA KRISHNAN

https://thedreampedlar.com/books/

Dying Wishes

Finalist, 2023 Rakuten Kobo Emerging Writer Prize in Speculative Fiction

A contemporary fantasy novel weaving Hindu mythology and South Indian folklore into a quest for belonging across different worlds — the World of Mortals and the World of Gods, India and Canada, the past and the present, the world outside and the one within.

Erased from Existence

A paranormal mystery in which a fifteen-year-old is erased from the memories and perception of everyone. Trapped in oblivion, she will have to unearth and reveal long-buried family secrets to escape.

The Land of No Reflection

A fantasy tale of two sightless young women on the run from their homeland, having committed the unpardonable crime of seeing.

A Benevolent Goddess

A story of a goddess who is punished for her desire to help human beings but is unable to find salvation by any other means.

In Search of Leo

A fantasy tale exploring the gamut of emotions that loss and grief can stir.

The Mind Meddler

A fantasy short story on the games The Mind Meddler plays by sneaking thoughts into people's minds, until he meets the one person who can resist his unkind mischief.

Mrs. D'Souza's Dispute With God

A fantasy short story in which a school teacher, Mrs. D'Souza, dies unexpectedly and sets out in search of God to demand answers to her burning questions on life and death.

Hello, Dreamer! Poems & Dreams

An eclectic collection of 100 short poems encompassing musings on the universe and its mysteries, nature and human life, my secret longings and fears, love and heartbreak, the sun and the moon, the stars and the seas, light and shadow, and joy and nostalgia.

ABOUT THE AUTHOR

Anitha Krishnan is a speculative fiction author and an award-winning poet. Her fantasy novel, *Dying Wishes*, was a finalist for the 2023 Rakuten Kobo Emerging Writer Prize in the Speculative Fiction category.

She has lived in and left pieces of her heart in many places across the world including Singapore, Australia, Canada, and most of all in her beloved birthplace, India. She presently lives in Burlington, Ontario with her husband and their cherished child.

Find more books and her blog on the writing life at
https://thedreampedlar.com.

Sign up to her monthly newsletter at
https://thedreampedlar.com/newsletter
to receive heartfelt musings, exclusive updates, book
recommendations, free fiction, and more!